THE RULES OF POKER

THE RULES OF
POKER

INTERNATIONAL
FEDERATION
OF POKER

First published in 2012 by IFP Books
An imprint of Limehouse Books Limited
Flat 30, 58 Glasshouse Fields, London E1W 3AB

Cover design by Katrina Clark
Typeset by Emily Foster
Printed in the UK by CPI Group (UK) Ltd, Croydon CR0 4YY

ISBN 978-1908781000

Distributed in UK and EU by Turnaround
Distributed in North America by SCB Distributors

www.pokerfed.org
www.limehousebooks.co.uk

CONTENTS

Preface

Soon after I was first elected President of the International Federation of Poker (IFP) in April 2009, David Flusfeder surprised me by volunteering for the potentially thankless task of chairing IFP's Rules Committee. Knowing this to be an especially vexed and contentious area, about which David is one of those players who cares passionately, I was more than content to run the idea by my IFP colleagues. Also knowing David to be a man of even temper, and a writer of scrupulous elegance – as the London *Sunday Telegraph*'s then poker columnist, and the author of several fine novels – I was also happy to give him my personal endorsement. I could think of no-one better equipped to adjudicate the thorniest disputes that can arise in the heat of a hand of poker, be it during a Friday night home game or a major international tournament.

As well as recruiting other experts of international prominence to serve alongside him, David and I consulted other previous compilers of poker rules, who were extremely helpful and generous with their time and expertise. Marcel Luske, poker's very own 'Flying Dutchman', has long been passionately vocal about the standardization of international tournament rules, and the Tournament Directors Association (TDA) of the United States has also produced its own magisterial, ever-evolving document. Martin Sturc, President of IFP's member federation from Austria, the Austrian Poker Sport Association (APSA), handed over APSA's own rulebook for translation into English by Matthew Johnson. These and others thanked in David's acknowledgments kindly put all their work at IFP's disposal.

But this book is designed to cover far more than merely tournament poker. It is the perfect volume to keep on hand in poker clubs and at kitchen-table home games the world over. As new areas of dispute arise, and fresh controversies develop, it will continue to evolve online, at IFP's website, and in paperback editions in future years. IFP's Rules Committee will continue to meet regularly to review all poker rulings, online and off, as the extraordinary 21st century 'boom' in this Mind Sport of strategic skill is further boosted by the arrival of its own governing Federation, with its own regular tournaments.

The book also covers more than merely Texas hold 'em, the relatively recent variant in poker's two-hundred-year history that has come to dominate the international tournament circuit and its television coverage. Explanations of all five components of H.O.R.S.E, generally regarded as the supreme test of the all-round poker player, can also be found in detail in these pages.

As can an exciting new variant of poker, pioneered by the IFP's executive director, Oliver Chubb, for both team and individual events, which many top professionals are already hailing as the supreme test of poker skill. Match Poker, in which the same hand is dealt simultaneously at different tables, offers a unique chance to test your own skill against those of others playing the same cards against the same cards in the same positions. If there is an element of luck in poker, in other words, Match Poker renders it the same for every player. "I guess that if luck weren't involved," pokerbrat Phil Hellmuth once famously declared to a TV camera, "then I'd win every hand." Match Poker gives Phil a chance, in short, to put his money where his mouth is.

In the presence of IFP's eminent Ambassador for Match Poker, James McManus, this new variant was first played publicly as a team event at the UK Festival of Mind Sports in November 2011, organized in London by IFP and the UK Mind Sports Association, under the experienced leadership of Don Morris. This was the first of a series of annual events designed to support and symbolize IFP's mission to have poker separated from gambling legislation, and regarded by governments and sports fans alike as a Mind Sport in the same respectable category as chess, bridge, draughts, Go, Chinese chess (Xiangqi) and its other partners in the International Mind Sports Association, of which IFP secured provisional membership in Dubai in 2010. This was the first step along the road to realizing our ultimate dream of Olympic recognition, also symbolized by Match Poker's participation in the 2012 World Mind Sports Games in the wake of the London Olympics.

Captain of the UK Match Poker team at both events was that genial and popular professional Barny Boatman, who has generously given the editor access to the archive of the Hendon Mob's savvy series *You Are The Tournament Director*, in which some of the most frequent or controversial disputes at the poker table are resolved by experts.

Add a definitive glossary of poker terminology, and you have a book which will be as invaluable to the poker rookie (as in the basic Laws of Poker, as opposed to the Rules) as much as the seasoned veteran in need of a fair and balanced ruling. This is, I believe, the only volume in print setting out the Rules of Poker. That it also offers so much more, making a huge contribution to the rich literature of the Mind Sport we all love, is a source of great pride to IFP, the game's global governing body, and to me personally as its President.

Anthony Holden
President, International Federation of Poker

Preamble

Poker needs rules. And it needs unified rules. There are variations, from country to country, or even from card room to card room. One can cross the Strip in Las Vegas and find that different procedures apply. A player should know exactly what is allowed and what isn't.

Previous rulebooks have been written as aids to Tournament Directors, to card rooms; these rules are written with players in mind, for play to be as smooth and uninterrupted as possible.

The spirit of common sense should prevail, so the ultimate arbiter in tournament disputes is the Tournament Director, who may make decisions against some of the "technical" rulings given here, in the greater interest of sportsmanship and fair play. The Tournament Director's decisions are final.

Poker is rare, perhaps unique, among sports and other games of skill in that players are acting in response to events that have already happened. The deck of cards has been shuffled and cut. Over the course of the hand, the cards are gradually revealed. So, one of the principles governing this rulebook is that, in the event of irregularities or dealer errors, the means of rectifying those will be to disturb as little as possible the arrangement of the cards.

There is a lot of hope, fear and aggression as well as money at the card table. A universally accepted rule book will, it is hoped, increase the chances of the game being played in its customary spirit of courtesy and good humor.

David Flusfeder
Chairman of Rules Committee,
International Federation of Poker

INTERNATIONAL FEDERATION OF POKER RULES FOR TOURNAMENT PLAY

IFP Rules Committee:

David Flusfeder (UK/US) Chairman
Devanir Campos (Brazil)
Roy Houghton (UK)
Thomas Kremser (Austria)
James McManus (US)

General Rules

1 **Tournament Director and Floor People**
Floor people are to consider sportsmanship and fairness as the top priorities in the decision-making process. Unusual circumstances can on occasion dictate that decisions in the interest of fairness take priority over the technical rules. The Tournament Director's (TD's) decisions are final.

2 **Official Language**
English will be used in international play along with the local or native language.

3 **Official Terminology of Tournament Poker**
Official terms are such straightforward and unambiguous declarations as: bet, raise, call, fold, check, all-in, pot (in pot-limit only). Regional terms may also meet this standard. The use of non-standard language is made at the player's risk and may result in an outcome – and a ruling – contrary to what the player intended. It is the responsibility of players to make their intentions clear.

4 **Communication Devices**
Players may not talk on the phone while at the poker table. Players who do so may incur a penalty

and have their hand killed. House rules apply to all other forms of electronic devices. Players wishing to talk on a cell phone must be at least one table length away from their assigned table during the communication.

Seating and Moving

5 **Random and Correct Tournament Seating**
Tournament and satellite seats will be randomly assigned. A player who started the tournament in the wrong seat with the correct chip stack amount will be moved to the correct seat along with his/her current total chip stack.

6 **Special Needs**
Accommodations for players with special needs will be made where possible.

7 **At Your Seat**
A player must be sitting at his/her seat by the time all players have been dealt complete initial hands to have a live hand.

Players must remain at the table if they still have action pending on a live hand. If a player leaves the table before he/she has acted on the hand, a penalty may be enforced when the player returns to the table.

8 **Absent Player**
An absent player will be dealt in and maintain his/her obligation for blinds, antes and forced bets. An

absent all-in hand will be automatically mucked and the player will be eliminated. The player will be entitled to any prize monies that finishing position may award.

9 Dead Stacks

At close of registration, any unsold seat's starting stack will be removed and the chips taken out of play.

10 Breaking Tables

Players going from a broken table to fill in seats assume the rights and responsibilities of the new position. They can get the big blind or the button. The only place they cannot get a hand is on the small blind or when occupying an empty seat between the small blind and the button. If the moved player is placed in that position, he/she will have to wait to play until the button has passed to him/her.

11 Balancing Tables

a. In flop and mixed games when balancing tables, the player who will be big blind next will be moved to the worst position, including taking a single big blind when available, even if that means the seat will have the big blind twice. Worst position is never the small blind. In stud-only events, players will be moved by position (the last seat to open up at the short table is the seat to be filled). The table from which a player is moved will be specified by a predetermined procedure. Play will halt on any table that is 3 or more players short.

b. In mixed games (example: H.O.R.S.E.), when the game shifts from hold 'em to stud, after the last hold 'em hand the button is moved exactly to the position it would be if the next hand was hold 'em and then frozen there during the stud round. The player moved during stud is the player who would be the big blind if the game was hold 'em for that hand. When hold 'em resumes, the button for the first hand will be at the position where it was frozen.

12 Dodging Blinds

Players who intentionally dodge any blind when moving from a broken table will incur a penalty.

13 Transporting Chips

Players may not hold or transport tournament chips in a manner that takes them out of view. Players who do so will forfeit the hidden chips and may be liable for disqualification. The forfeited chips will be taken out of play.

14 Multi-Day Tournaments

In a tournament that continues over multiple days, the clock will be stopped within the last fifteen minutes of the final level of the day and the last three to seven hands will be announced instead.

The time will be decided by the Tournament Director and the number of hands decided randomly by an active player in the tournament, or at the discretion of the TD.

15 Final Table

When the final table is reached, players must have a random redraw for seats.

THE TABLE

16 Random Draw for the Button

The starting position of the dealer button starting position will be randomly drawn.

17 Dead Button

Tournament play will use a "dead button" – if the player who was to have the button is eliminated, the button will go to the vacant seat and the blinds posted as if there had been no elimination.

18 Button in Heads-Up

In heads-up play, the small blind is on the button and acts first pre-flop and last on all subsequent betting rounds. The last card is dealt to the button. When beginning heads-up play, the button may need to be adjusted to ensure no player takes the big blind twice in a row.

19 Single Big Blind

If the player who was to post the small blind is eliminated, there will be a single big blind (no player can post the same blind twice).

20 Cards Visible

Players must keep their cards in view at all times on

the table. Cards should not be completely covered by players' hands or concealed by a card protector.

21 Chips Visibility

Players' chips must be visible at all times. Higher denomination chips must be clearly displayed at the front or top of the player's chip stack. Players are entitled to a reasonable estimation of an opponent's chip count; thus chips should be kept in countable stacks. The IFP recommends clean stacks in multiples of twenty as a standard. TDs will control the number and denomination of chips in play and may color up at their discretion. Discretionary color-ups are to be announced.

22 Foreign Objects

There are to be no foreign objects on the table except for a maximum of one card protector per player. Electronic devices are not permitted to be placed on the table.

ACTION

23 New Hand and New Limits

When time has elapsed in a round and a new level is announced by a member of the tournament staff, the new level applies to the next hand. A hand begins with the first riffle. If an automatic shuffler is being used, the hand begins when the green button is pressed.

24 Disputed Pots

The right to dispute a hand ends when a new hand begins.

25 Action in Turn

Verbal declarations of action or physical declarations of action made with an intentional movement of chips are binding. Players must act in turn at all times.

26 Action Out of Turn

Action out of turn, whether the declaration is verbal or physical, will be binding if the action to that player has not changed. A check, call or fold is not considered action-changing. If a player acts out of turn and the action changes, the person who acted out of turn may change his/her action by calling, raising or folding and may have his/her chips returned. Players may not intentionally act out of turn to influence play before them. Violators will receive a penalty. An out-of-turn fold is binding.

27 Accidentally Killed/Fouled Hand

Players must protect their own hands at all times. If a dealer kills a hand by mistake, or a hand is fouled, the player will have no redress and is not entitled to a refund of bets. If the player initiated a bet or raise and has not been called, the uncalled bet or raise will be returned to the player.

28 Non-Standard Folds

Folding in turn when facing a check or folding out of turn are both binding folds and may be subject to penalty.

29 Substantial Action

Substantial action is defined as either:
a. Any two actions in turn, at least one of which must involve putting chips in the pot (i.e. any two actions except two checks or two folds); or
b. Any combination of three actions in turn (check, bet, raise, call, or fold).

30 Accepted Action

Poker is a game of alert, continuous observation. It is the caller's responsibility to determine the correct amount of an opponent's bet before calling, regardless of what is stated by the dealer or players. If a caller requests a count but receives incorrect information from the dealer or players, then places that amount in the pot, the caller is assumed to accept the full correct action and is subject to the correct wager or all-in amount. As with all tournament situations, Rule #1 may apply at the TD's discretion.

Betting and Raising

31 Making a Bet

A bet can be announced verbally or made physically, with a movement of chips. In the event of a player making a verbal and a physical declaration, whichever occurs first will be binding. Any chips that are moved in a significant forward motion, whether or not they touch the table, will be deemed a bet.

32 Raising a Bet

In no-limit or pot-limit, a raise must be made by:

a. Placing the full amount in the pot in one motion;

b. Verbally declaring the full amount prior to the initial placement of chips into the pot;

c. Verbally declaring "raise" prior to the placement of the amount to call into the pot and then completing the action with one additional motion. It is the player's responsibility to make his/her intentions clear.

33 Number of Allowable Raises

There is no cap on the number of raises in no-limit and pot-limit play. In limit events there will be a limit to one bet and three raises, even when heads-up, until the tournament is down to two players.

34 Use of a Single Oversized Chip

Anytime when facing a bet or blind, placing a single oversized chip in the pot is a call if a raise isn't first verbally declared. To raise with an oversized chip, the raise must be declared before the chip hits the table surface. If raise is declared (but no amount), the raise is the maximum allowable for that chip. When not facing a bet, placing an oversized chip in the pot without declaration is a bet of the maximum for the chip.

35 Using Multiple Chips of the Same Value

When facing a bet, unless a raise is first declared, multiple same-denomination chips is a call if removing one chip leaves less than the call amount. Example of a call: pre-flop, blinds are 200-400: Player A raises to 1200 total (an 800 raise), Player B puts out two 1000 chips without declaring raise. This is just a call because removing one 1000 chip leaves less than the amount needed to call the 1200 bet. Placing mixed denomination chips in the pot is governed by the **Raise Requirements** rule #37.

36 String Betting

Chips placed in the pot in multiple movements, without a prior verbal declaration, will be considered a string bet, and only the chips committed in the first movement will be allowable and will follow the raising and betting minimum value rules. Dealers will be responsible for permitting or rejecting string bets and raises.

37 Raise Requirements

a. A raise must be at least the size of the largest previous bet, or raise of the current betting round. If a player puts in an amount of chips that is 150% or more of the previous bet, then he/she will be required to make a full minimum raise.

b. An all-in bet of less than a full raise does not reopen the betting to a player who has already acted in that same betting round. Players left to act may still re-raise the original bet.

38 Non-Standard and Unclear Betting

Players use unofficial vocabulary and gestures at their own risk. These may be interpreted to mean other than what the player intended. Also, whenever the size of a declared bet can have multiple meanings, it will be ruled as having the smallest legitimate value. (Example: "I bet five". If it is unclear whether "five" means $500 or $5,000, the bet stands as $500).

39 Pot Size and Pot-Limit Bets

Players are entitled to be informed of the pot size in pot-limit games only. Dealers will not count the pot in limit and no-limit games. Declaring "I bet the pot" is not a valid bet in no-limit but it does bind the player to making a bet. Players may ask the dealer to spread the pot for them to enable them to see it more clearly.

40 Raise Value

Players are not to be informed automatically by the dealer of the raise size (difference between last bet and current raise) – in other words, how much more is the call. Players will be informed of the raise size by the dealer upon request.

41 All-In Betting

Players betting all-in must clearly declare their action and/or move an obvious amount of their entire chip stack forward. An all-in bet commits a player's entire chip stack to the hand. Discovered or hidden chips will be committed to the pot.

POTS AND SHOWDOWNS

42 Showdown Order

In a non-all-in showdown, at the end of the final round of betting, the player who made the last aggressive action in that betting round must show first. If there was no bet in the last round, the player to the left of the button shows first and so on in a clockwise direction. In stud, the player with the high board must show first. In razz, the lowest board shows first.

43 Face-Up for All-Ins

When one or more players is all-in and all betting action by all the players in the hand are complete, the dealer will instruct the players to turn their cards face-up.

44 Uncontested Showdown

At showdown, when all opponents have mucked their hands, the last live hand wins the pot.

45 Playing the Board at Showdown

A player must show all hole cards when playing the board in order to get part of the pot.

46 Killing a Winning Hand

Dealers cannot kill a winning hand that was tabled and was obviously the winning hand. Players are encouraged to assist in reading tabled hands if it appears that an error is about to be made or has been made.

47 Asking to See a Hand at Showdown

Except where house policy requires a hand to be shown or provides an express right to see a hand on request, asking to see a hand is a privilege granted at the TD's discretion to protect the integrity of the game (suspicion of invalid hand, collusion, etc). This privilege is not to be abused. A player who mucks his hand face-down at showdown without fully tabling it loses any rights he may have to ask to see any hand.

48 Declarations at Showdown

Verbal declarations as to the contents of a player's hand at showdown are not binding. Even if the player has miscalled the hand, the value of the cards tabled speak for themselves. However, any player deliberately miscalling his/her hand may be penalized.

49 Valid Hand

The winning player must have the correct number of cards in an unfouled deck to win the pot.

50 Awarding Odd Chips

In high-low games the odd chip goes to the high hand. In flop games when there are two or more high hands or two or more low hands, the odd chip(s) will go to the left of the button. In stud, the odd chip goes to the high card by suit.

51 Side Pots

In the event of a side pot or pots, each pot must be dealt with separately, starting with the most recent side pot and ending with the main pot. Each side pot will be split separately.

52 Folded Hands

A hand is considered folded upon being touched to the "muck": the burn cards, the board, or the discard pile while face-down, either by the player or the dealer. Utilizing Rule #1, the Floor Person may retrieve a technically mucked hand and declare it live if he/she believes there is good cause to do so and the correct hand is clearly retrievable.

53 Dead Hands in Stud

In stud poker, if a player picks up the up cards while facing action, the hand is dead.

GENERAL PROCEDURES

54 Deck Changes
Deck changes will be on the dealer push or level changes or as prescribed by the house. Players may not ask for deck changes unless they find cards that have been damaged or marked.

55 Calling for a Clock
Once a reasonable amount of time has passed and a clock is called for by any player sitting at the table, the player to act will be given a maximum of one minute to make a decision. If action has not been taken before time expires, there will be a ten-second countdown followed by a declaration to the effect that the hand is dead. If the player has not acted before the declaration, the hand is dead.

56 Chip Race
When it is time to color-up chips, they will be raced off with a maximum of one chip going to any player. The chip race will always start in the No.1 seat. Chips will be changed to the next higher denomination in play and an odd number of chips will be rounded up (50% or more) or down (less than 50%). A player cannot be raced out of a tournament: a player who loses his remaining

chip(s) in a chip race will be given one chip of the smallest denomination still in play. Players are encouraged to witness the chip race.

57 Eliminated Players

Players eliminated on the same hand at different tables will "tie" for that finishing position and prize money. Players eliminated on the same hand at the same table will have their finishing position determined by chip count at the start of the elimination hand: the player who had the lower chip count going into the hand will be considered to have been eliminated first. Eliminated players must vacate their seats immediately. No-one not in the tournament may sit at or by a tournament table.

58 Rabbit Hunting

No "rabbit hunting" is allowed. After the pot is awarded, the dealer will gather the cards in preparation for the next hand. Rabbit hunting is defined as showing any further cards that would have been dealt or revealed if the hand had not ended.

59 Rebuys and Add-ons

In rebuy tournaments, if a player is eligible to rebuy, he/she may rebuy as long as it is done before the next hand is dealt. If the player announces the intent to rebuy without immediately receiving chips, that player is playing chips behind and is obligated to make the rebuy. The rebuying player must present the funds before receiving the chips.

60 Tournament Payouts

The tournament staff must have the payout structure readily available to all players.

61 Hand-for-Hand

As tournaments near the "money", the TD may dictate hand-for-hand play as the method of determining player placement, in which each hand is begun simultaneously at all tables. (The TD may also dictate that each street be dealt simultaneously). If a player is "all-in" and facing a showdown while playing hand-for-hand, the hand will be stopped, and continued when all the hands on other tables are finished.

62 Deal-Making

If the tournament rules permit deal-making between remaining players at the final table, players may choose to discuss a new arrangement for the disposal of prize money. Agreement must be unanimous. If a deal is reached, players must immediately inform the TD. Any player who attempts to constrain, coerce or force another disagreeing player will receive a penalty and the deal will be deemed void.

DEALING/DECK IRREGULARITIES

63 Fouled Deck

The hand will be declared void if at any time during the hand, the deck is discovered to have:

a. Too few or too many cards;

b. Cards with different colored backs;

c. Two or more cards of the same suit and rank.

Any player knowing or noticing that the deck is fouled has an obligation to bring this immediately to the attention of the dealer. A player using this information for advantage will be subject to a penalty or disqualification. A player intentionally fouling the deck will be disqualified.

64 Misdeal

If a misdeal is declared, all bets will be returned to players, and the action voided. Once substantial action has occurred (see above, Rule #28), a misdeal cannot be declared and the hand must be played out. Misdeal situations include but are not necessarily limited to:

a. The first or second card of the hand are dealt up or exposed through dealer error;

b. Two or more hole cards have been exposed by the dealer;

c. Two or more "boxed" cards are found;

d. Two or more extra cards have been dealt;
e. An incorrect number of cards have been dealt to a player;
f. Any card is dealt out of its proper sequence (except an exposed card that may be used as the burn card);
g. A player's initial card has been mixed with another player's card;
h. The dealer button was at the wrong position;
i. The first card is dealt to the wrong seat;
j. Cards have been dealt to an empty seat or to a player not entitled to a hand;
k. A player who is entitled to a hand has been dealt out;
l. The deck is discovered to have been fouled.

65 Board Irregularities
Please refer to the Appendix.

ETIQUETTE, ETHICAL PLAY AND PENALTIES

66 One Player to a Hand

Players are obligated to protect other players in the tournament and maintain the fairness of the action at all times. Therefore, players, whether in the hand or not, may not:

a. Disclose contents of live or folded hands;
b. Advise or criticise play during the play of a hand;
c. Read a hand that hasn't been tabled.

The one-player-to-a-hand rule will be enforced.

67 Exposing Cards

A player who exposes his/her cards with action pending may incur a penalty, but will not have a dead hand. The penalty will begin at the end of the hand.

68 Conditional Statements

Conditional statements regarding future action are non-standard and strongly discouraged; they may be binding and/or subject to penalty at the TD's discretion. (Example: "if–then" statements such as "If you bet, then I will raise").

69 Checking "the nuts"

Poker is a game of aggressive action. If on the last

round of betting the last player to act checks or calls with the best possible hand for the board being played, that will be considered a form of soft play and a penalty may be enforced.

70 **Penalties and Disqualification**

A penalty may be invoked if the player violates any rules or behaves in an unethical and unsportsmanlike way. Penalties available to the TD include verbal warnings, "missed hand" penalties, and disqualification. Except for a one-hand penalty, missed hand penalties will be assessed as follows: The offender will miss one hand for every player, including the offender, who is at the table when the penalty is given, multiplied by the number of rounds specified in the penalty. For the period of the penalty, the offender shall remain away from the table but will continue to be dealt in. Tournament staff can assess a one-hand penalty, one-, two-, three-, or four-orbit penalties or disqualification. A player who is disqualified shall have his/her chips removed from play. Repeat infractions are subject to escalating penalties.

71 **Ethical Play**

Poker is an individual game. Actions, statements or conduct detrimental to the progress of fair competition, whether intended or not, are considered unethical and unsporting. The TD will prioritize the competitive integrity of the tournament and, therefore, punish any contestant who cheats or acts unethically or illegally.

Cheating is defined as deliberately breaking the rules of the tournament to gain an advantage. Cheating may include, but is not limited to, collusion, theft of chips, transfer of chips between participants in the same tournament or separate events, marking cards, substituting replacement cards or use of any other unauthorised methods or equipment.

Collusion is defined as the agreement between two or more competitors to share information and play together to achieve an advantage in the tournament. Collusion includes, but is not limited to, chip dumping (passing chips), soft play, sharing information about cards with another competitor, sending or receiving signals to/from another competitor, using electronic or other aids to exchange information.

72 Behavior and Etiquette

In order to maintain a congenial environment for all players, the TD may, at his/her sole discretion, penalize, suspend or disqualify a participant who acts in the following ways, but not limited to:

a. Acting out of turn intentionally and/or repeatedly;
b. Intentionally folding and/or placing cards in the

muck out of turn, including leaving the table before it is his/her turn to act;

c. Intentionally and/or repeatedly miscalling hands at the showdown;

d. Intentionally and/or repeatedly exposing hole cards with action pending in the table;

e. Intentionally and/or repeatedly slowing down the tempo of the game by taking too long to act;

f. Violating the "one player to a hand" rule, including discussion about a hand with a competitor or observer while the hand is in progress;

g. Revealing mucked cards while a hand is being played;

h. Any form of soft play, including verbal or clear agreement to "check all the way" when a third player is all-in;

i. Directing or controlling the action of another player;

j. Intentionally and/or repeatedly splashing chips into the pot;

k. Throwing cards off the table, at the dealer, or at another player in an aggressive and/or abusive manner; intentionally and/or repeatedly destroying or damaging cards; damaging any property of other players; or damaging the property of the organizers of the event;

l. Adopting abusive and harassing behavior, including excessive celebrations;

m. Wearing any clothing or other materials that carry words or images that display derogatory, offensive, racist, illegal or aggressive messages;

n. Using masks or objects that hide the identity of a player;

o. Intentionally and/or repeatedly touching the cards or chips of another competitor;

p. Verbally or physically attacking other competitors, members of the tournament staff or spectators;

q. Displaying signs of alcohol intoxication, drunkenness or use of other substances that jeopardizes the smooth running of the tournament or causes disrespect to other competitors, staff or spectators;

r. Displaying unsocial conditions of hygiene, including excessive body odor or dirt that jeopardizes other players' right to a pleasant and safe environment.

73 Dress Code

In official IFP events, players may not wear hats, hoods or sunglasses or any garment or device (except for religious reasons) that obscures any part of the face. Smart-casual attire is required: shorts and sleeveless tops, and open shoes, such as sandals and flip-flops, are not to be worn. Players may not use any device to insulate themselves from the sounds of the game, including but not limited to ear-plugs, personal stereos and noise-cancelling headphones.

Appendix: Board Irregularities

I. Board Errors on the Flop

Prematurely exposed cards
All flopped cards and burn card(s), excluding discards, will be returned to the deck. The cards will be reshuffled. After the betting round is completed, the dealer will shuffle the cards, cut the deck, burn a card, and deal a new flop.

No burn card – no player has acted
The TD will try to reset the flop in the correct way; if this is not possible, all flopped cards will be returned to the deck, excluding discards. The cards will be reshuffled. The dealer will cut the deck, burn a card, and deal a new flop.

No burn card – at least one player has acted
The flopped cards must stand; and betting continues. The subsequent cards should be those that would have come as if no error had occurred. The dealer will burn two consecutive cards before dealing the turn.

Too many burn cards – no player has acted
All flopped cards will be returned to the deck. The deck, excluding discards, will be reshuffled. The dealer

will cut the deck, burn a card, and deal a new flop.

Too many burn cards – at least one player has acted
The flopped cards must stand; and betting continues. The subsequent cards should be those that would have come as if no error had occurred. The dealer will deal the turn without burning a card.

Too many board cards – no player has acted
If the dealer accidentally deals four cards on the flop and the additional card is 100% identifiable, the additional card will be deemed an exposed burn card and play will continue. After the betting round is completed, the dealer will deal the turn card without burning a card.

If the flop cards are not 100% identifiable, all four flopped cards will be turned face-down and shuffled among themselves. A new flop will be dealt using three of the four exposed cards, the additional card will be treated as an exposed burn card and play will continue.

II. Board Errors on the Turn

Prematurely exposed cards
The exposed card will be put to one side and once the betting round is completed, the dealer will shuffle the remaining deck with the exposed turn card and deal a new turn card.

No burn card – no player has acted
The turned card will be deemed an exposed card and used as the burn card. The subsequent cards will be used as if no mistake had been made.

No burn card – at least one player has acted
The turn card must stand. The dealer will burn two consecutive cards before dealing the river.

Too many burn cards – no player has acted
If the correct turn card is 100% identifiable, then that should be replaced for the exposed card. After the betting round is complete, the dealer will deal the river without burning a card.

If the turn card is not 100% identifiable, then the burn cards and exposed card will stand. After the betting round is complete, the dealer will deal the river without burning a card.

Too many burn cards – at least one player has acted
The burn cards and turn card must stand. After the

betting round is complete, the dealer will deal the river without burning a card.

Too many board cards – no player has acted
If the correct turn card is 100% identifiable, then that should be used; the exposed extra card will be used as the burn card for the river. After the betting round is completed, the dealer will deal the river card without burning a card.

If the correct turn card is not 100% identifiable, the exposed turn cards will be shuffled with the deck and a new turn card will be dealt without burning another card.

Too many board cards – at least one player has acted
If the correct turn card is 100% identifiable, then that should be used; the exposed extra card will be used as the burn card for the river. After the betting round is completed; the dealer will deal the river card without burning a prior card.

If the correct turn card is not 100% identifiable, the exposed turn cards will be shuffled with the deck and a new turn card will be dealt without burning another card.

III. Board Errors on the River

Prematurely exposed cards
The exposed river card will be taken out of play and betting completed. After the betting round is completed, the dealer will reshuffle the deck, including the exposed river card but excluding burn cards and discards. The dealer will then cut the deck and deal a new river card without burning a card.

No burn card – no player has acted
The exposed card will be used as the burn card. A new river card will be turned.

No burn card – at least one player has acted
The river card must stand.

Too many burn cards – no player has acted
If the correct river card is 100% identifiable, it will be revealed and the incorrectly turned river card will be deemed an exposed card and discarded.

If the correct river card is not 100% identifiable, the burn cards and river will stand.

Too many burn cards – at least one player has acted
The burn cards and river will stand.

Too many board cards – no player has acted
If the correct river card is 100% identifiable, it will be

revealed and the incorrectly turned river card will be deemed an exposed card and discarded.

If the correct river card is not 100% identifiable, the dealer will reshuffle the deck, including the exposed river cards, but excluding the burn cards and discards. The dealer then cuts the deck, burns a card and deals the river card.

Too many board cards – at least one player has acted

If the correct river card is 100% identifiable, it will be revealed and the incorrectly turned river card will be deemed an exposed card and discarded.

If the correct river card is not 100% identifiable, the dealer will reshuffle the deck, including the exposed river cards, but excluding the burn cards and discards. The dealer then cuts the deck, burns a card and deals the river card.

Variations and Considerations For Cash Play

Cash games must always be played for table stakes: you may only bet what you have in front of you. Players may not add to their chip stack during a hand. More can be added before the start of a hand. Conversely, players may not remove chips from their stack, either to put them away or to pass them. Money that has been won must stay in the game, in the stack of the player who won it. (The only exception is in a card room, to buy food or drink to consume at the table, and to tip waiting staff).

Players, even at the smallest home games, are strongly encouraged to use chips rather than cash to wager with. As the Vegas sage said, "The guy who invented money was smart. The guy who invented chips was a genius."

Rules of Poker Variants

Board games

Texas Hold 'Em

Each player is dealt two hole cards. There is a round of betting. The top card of the remaining deck is discarded (burned) and the first three communal cards (the flop) are revealed, followed by a round of betting. The next card is burned, and the fourth card (the turn) is revealed, followed by a round of betting. The next card is burned, and the final board card (the river) is revealed, followed by a round of betting. In the event of a showdown, the best five-card hand, using any combination of hole cards and the board, is awarded the pot.

Irish (aka Pineapple)

Each player is dealt three cards (or more, if the table agrees). There is a round of betting. After the flop is dealt and before the next round of betting, players discard their extra cards so each has two hole cards, and the game proceeds as in hold 'em.

Omaha

Omaha is similar to hold 'em in using a three-card flop on the board, a fourth board card, and then a fifth board card. But, each player is dealt four hole cards at the start. In order to make a hand, a player must use precisely two hole cards with three board cards. The betting is the same as in hold 'em. At the showdown, the entire five-card hand should be shown to receive the pot, and all four hole cards must be shown.

Omaha High-Low

Omaha is often played high-low split, in which the highest hand and the lowest hand split the pot. Players may use any combination of two hole cards and three board cards for the high hand and another (or the same) combination of two hole cards and three board cards for the low hand.

To qualify for the low pot, a player's hand at the showdown must contain five cards of different value that are eight or lower in rank. (An ace can play as the highest card and also the lowest card). If there is no qualifying hand for low, the best high hand scoops the whole pot.

Straights and flushes do not impair the low value of a hand.

Chinese Poker

Each player receives a thirteen-card hand, which he/she then arranges into a "setting" of three distinct hands: two contain five-card hands, the "middle" and the "back". The third, the "front", contains a three-card hand.

The back must be the highest ranking hand, and the front, the lowest ranking hand (straights and flushes do not count in the three-card hand). The back hand is placed face-down on the table in front of the player, then the middle hand is placed face-down in front of the back hand, and the front hand is placed face-down in front of the middle hand. After all the players have set their hands, each player will announce in turn (clockwise, starting from the left of the dealer) whether or not he/she is playing the hand. All players then announce their royalties before revealing their hands.

If a player makes three flushes or three straights he/she automatically wins the hand, regardless of the other players' hands.

The two most common scoring systems used in Chinese poker are the 2-4 scoring method, and the 1-6 scoring method:

In the 2-4 method the player receives one unit for each of the three hands he/she wins—as well as the overall unit awarded to the player who wins the majority or all of the hands. In the event of a tie in one of the hands, no money is exchanged for this particular hand. If one player wins both of the other two hands, he/she collects three units (one for each hand, and one overall). If they each win one hand, no units are exchanged (each win one unit, and there is no overall winner).

In the 1-6 method the winning player receives one unit for each of the three hands he/she wins, and three bonus units (on top of the three for the hands) if he/she wins all three hands.

STUD GAMES

Seven-Card Stud

Seven-Card Stud is played with a starting hand of two down cards and one up card dealt before the first betting round. There are then three more up cards and a final down card, with a betting round after each, for a total of five betting rounds on a deal played to the showdown. The best five-card poker hand wins the pot. In all fixed-limit games, the smaller bet is wagered for the first two betting rounds, and the larger bet is wagered for the last three betting rounds (on the fifth, sixth, and seventh cards). If there is an open pair on the fourth card, any player has the option of making the smaller or larger bet. Deliberately changing the order of your up cards in a stud game is improper because it unfairly misleads the other players.

1. If your first or second hole card is accidentally turned up by the dealer, then your third card will be dealt down. If both hole cards are dealt up, you have a dead hand and receive your ante back. If the first card dealt face-up would have been the lowcard, action starts with the first hand to that player's left. That player may fold, open for the forced bet, or open for

a full bet. (In tournament play, if a down card is dealt face-up, a misdeal is called).

2. The first round of betting starts with a forced bet by the lowest up card by suit. On subsequent betting rounds, the high hand initiates the action (a tie is broken by position, with the player who received cards first acting first).

3. The player with the forced bet has the option of opening for a full bet.

4. If the player with the low card is all-in for the ante, the person to that player's left acts first. If the player with the low card has only enough chips for a portion of the forced bet, all other players must enter for at least the normal amount.

5. When the wrong person is designated as low and bets, if the next player has not yet acted, the action will be corrected to the real low card, who now must bet. The incorrect low card takes back the bet. If the next hand has acted after the incorrect low card bets, the bet stands, action continues from there, and the real low card has no obligations.

6. Increasing the amount wagered by the opening forced bet up to a full bet does not count as a raise, but merely as a completion of the bet. For example: In $15-$30 stud, the low card opens for $5. If the next player

increases the bet to $15 (completes the bet), up to three raises are then allowed when using a three-raise limit.

7. In all fixed-limit games, when an open pair is showing on fourth street (second up card), any player has the option of betting either the lower or the upper limit. For example: In a $5-$10 game, if you have a pair showing and are the high hand, you may bet either $5 or $10. If you bet $5, any player then has the option to call $5, raise $5, or raise $10. If a $10 raise is made, then all other raises must be in increments of $10. If the high player with the open pair on fourth street checks, then subsequent players have the same options that were given to the player who was high.

8. If a hand is folded when there is no wager, that seat will continue to receive cards until the hand is killed as a result of a bet (so the fold does not affect who gets the cards to come).

9. When facing a bet, any player picking up his/her up cards without calling is deemed to have folded. This act has no significance at the showdown because betting is over; the hand is live until discarded.

10. A card dealt off the table is treated as an exposed card.

11. The dealer announces the low card, the high hand, all raises, and all pairs. Dealers do not announce

possible straights or flushes.

12. If the dealer burns two cards for one round or fails to burn a card, the cards will be corrected, if possible, to their proper positions. If this should happen on a final down card, and either a card intermingles with a player's other hole cards or a player looks at the card, the player must accept that card.

13. If the dealer burns and deals one or more cards before a round of betting has been completed, the card(s) must be eliminated from play. After the betting for that round is completed, an additional card for each remaining player still active in the hand is also eliminated from play. After that round of betting has concluded, the dealer burns a card and play resumes. The removed cards are held off to the side in the event the dealer runs out of cards. If the prematurely dealt card is the final down card and has been looked at or intermingled with the player's other hole cards, the player must keep the card, and on sixth street betting he/she may not bet or raise.

14. If there are not enough cards left in the deck for all players, all the cards are dealt except the last card, which is mixed with the burn cards (and any cards removed from the deck, as in the previous rule). The dealer then scrambles and cuts these cards, burns again, and delivers the remaining down cards, using the last card if necessary. If there are not as many cards as players

remaining without a card, the dealer does not burn, so that each player can receive a fresh card. If the dealer determines that there will not be enough fresh cards for all of the remaining players, then the dealer announces to the table that a common card will be used. The dealer will burn a card and turn one card face-up in the centre of the table as a common card that plays in everyone's hand. The player who is now high using the common card initiates the action for the last round.

15. An all-in player should receive hole cards dealt face-down, but if the final hole card to such a player is dealt face-up, the card must be kept, and the other players receive their normal card.

16. If the dealer turns the last card face-up to any player, the hand now high on the board using all the up cards will start the action. The following rules apply to the dealing of cards:

a. If there are more than two players, all remaining players receive their last card face-down. A player whose last card is face-up has the option of declaring all-in before betting action starts, meaning that the player does not put any more chips into the pot and subsequent betting by the other active players will be on the side.

b. If there are only two players remaining and the first player's final down card is dealt face-up, the second player's final down card will also be dealt face-up, and the betting proceeds as normal. In the event the first player's final card is dealt face-down and the opponent's final card is dealt face-up, the player with the face-up final card has the option of declaring all-in (before betting action starts).

17. A hand with more than seven cards is dead. A hand with less than seven cards at the showdown is dead, except any player missing a seventh card may have the hand ruled live.

Razz (Seven-Card Stud Low)

The lowest-ranking hand wins the pot. Aces are low only, and two aces are the lowest pair. The high card is required to make the forced bet on the first round; the low hand acts first on all subsequent rounds. Straights and flushes have no adverse effect on the low value of a hand, so the best possible hand is 5-4-3-2-A. An open pair does not affect the betting limit.

The highest card by suit starts the action with a forced bet. The low hand acts first on all subsequent rounds. If the low hand is tied, the first player clockwise from the dealer starts the action.

Fixed-limit games use the lower limit on third and fourth streets and the upper limit on subsequent streets. An open pair does not affect the limit.

Seven-Card Stud High-Low

A qualifier of eight-or-better for low applies to all high-low split games. To win for low, a player's hand at the showdown must have five cards of different ranks that are an eight or lower. If there is no qualifier for low, the best high hand scoops the whole pot. Any five cards may be used to make the best high hand, and the same or any other five cards to make the best low hand.

An ace is the highest card and also the lowest card.

The low card by suit initiates the action on the first round, with an ace counting as a high card for this purpose. On subsequent rounds, the high hand initiates the action. If the high hand is tied, the first player in the tie clockwise from the dealer acts first. If the high hand is all-in, action proceeds clockwise as if that person had checked.

Straights and flushes do not affect the value of a low hand.

Fixed-limit games use the lower limit on third and fourth streets and the upper limit on subsequent rounds. An open pair on fourth street does not affect the limit.

Cards Speak/Declarations

The awarding of pots in high-low games is made regardless of players' declarations. However, many home-games play high-low with a declaration at the end: the standard method is for the players in the showdown to take two chips off the table, and then to put no chips in their declaring hand to declare they're going for the low hand; one chip in the hand if they're going for high; two chips in the hand if they're going for both. Players involved in the showdown will reveal their declaration by opening their fists simultaneously (often after a countdown from three to zero). The pot will be split between the highest and lowest hand. In the event of identical qualifying hands, they will take equal shares of their half of the pot. If a player has declared both ways, he/she must win both outright ("scoop"): if there is a tie either way, the player forfeits both parts of the pot.

Superstud
A variant of Seven-Card Stud High-Low, in which each player is dealt five hole cards, of which they discard two. Simultaneously, they turn one card face-up; the game now follows the customary procedures of Seven-Card High-Low.

H.O.R.S.E.
H.O.R.S.E. poker is made up of five different games: Texas hold 'em; Omaha High-Low; Razz; Seven-Card Stud; Seven-Card Stud High-Low, Eight or better. (See above for rules of each of the variants).

H.O.R.S.E. is played as a limit game; except in the World Series of Poker (WSOP) event, at which the final table is exclusively no-limit hold 'em.

Draw Games

Draw High

There are two betting rounds, one before the draw and one after the draw. The game is played with a button and an ante. Players in turn may check, open for the minimum, or open with a raise. After the first betting round the players have the opportunity to draw new cards to replace the ones they discard. Action after the draw starts with the opener, or next player proceeding clockwise if the opener has folded. The betting limit after the draw is twice the amount of the betting limit before the draw. Some draw high games allow a player to open on anything; others require the opener to have a pair of jacks or better.

A maximum of a bet and four raises is permitted in multi-handed pots.

Check-raise is permitted both before and after the draw.

Any card that is exposed by the dealer before the draw must be kept.

Five cards constitute a playing hand. If action has been taken, a player with fewer than five cards may draw the number of cards necessary to complete a five-card hand. The button may receive the fifth card even if action has taken place. More or fewer than five cards after the draw constitutes a fouled hand.

A player may draw up to four consecutive cards. If a player wishes to draw five new cards, four are dealt right away, and the fifth card after everyone else has drawn cards. If the last player wishes to draw five new cards, four are dealt right away, and a card is burned before the player receives a fifth card.

Players may change the number of cards they wish to draw, provided:

a. No cards have been dealt off the deck in response to the original request (including the burn card);
b. No player has acted, in either the betting or indicating the number of cards to be drawn, based on the number of cards the first player has requested.

On the draw, an exposed card cannot be taken. The draw is completed to each player in order, and then the exposed card is replaced.

If a player is asked how many cards he/she drew by another active player, he/she is obliged to respond until there has been action after the draw, and the dealer is also obliged to respond. Once there is any action after the draw, the player is no longer obliged to respond and the dealer may not respond.

Rapping the table in turn constitutes either a pass or the declaration of a pat hand that does not want to draw any cards, depending on the situation. A player who indicates a pat hand by rapping the table, not knowing the pot has been raised, may still play his/her hand.

If the pot has been declared open by an all-in player playing for just the antes, all callers must come in for the full opening bet.

If you have only a full ante and no other chips on the table, you may play for just the antes. If no-one opens and there is another ante, you may still play for that part of the antes that you have matched, without putting in any more money.

The Joker

The joker may be used only as an ace, or to complete a straight, flush, or straight flush. (Thus it is not a completely wild card).

If the joker is used to make a flush, it will be the highest card of the flush not present in the hand.

Five aces is the best possible hand (four aces and joker).

Lowball

Lowball is draw poker with the lowest hand winning the pot. Each player is dealt five cards face-down, after which there is a betting round. Players are required to open with a bet or fold. The players who remain in the pot after the first betting round now have an option to improve their hand by replacing cards in their hands with new ones. The game is normally played with one or more blinds, sometimes with an ante added. Some betting structures allow the big blind to be called; other structures require the minimum open to be double the big blind. In limit poker, the usual structure has the limit double after the draw. The most popular forms of lowball are ace-to-five lowball (also known as California lowball), and deuce-to-seven lowball (also known as Kansas City lowball). Ace-to-five lowball gets its name because the best hand is 5-4-3-2-A. In deuce-to-seven lowball the best hand is 7-5-4-3-2 (not of the same suit).

In limit play, a bet and four raises are allowed in multi-handed pots.

A player may draw up to four consecutive cards. If a player wishes to draw five new cards, four are dealt right away, and the fifth card after everyone else has drawn cards. If the last player wishes to draw five new cards, four are dealt right away, and a card is burned before the player receives a fifth card.

Five cards constitute a playing hand. Before the draw, if a player has fewer than five cards in his/her hand, he/she may receive additional cards, provided no action has been taken by the first player to act. However, the dealer position may still receive a missing fifth card, even if action has taken place. If action has been taken, players are entitled on the draw to receive the number of cards necessary to complete a five-card hand.

Ace-to-Five Lowball
In ace-to-five lowball, the best hand is any 5-4-3-2-A (the "wheel"). An ace is the lowest-ranking card. For hands with a pair, A-A beats 2-2. Straights and flushes do not count against the hand.

If a joker is used, it becomes the lowest card not present in the hand.

In limit play, check-raise is not permitted.

Before the draw, an exposed card of seven or under must be taken, and an exposed card higher than a seven must be replaced after the deal has been completed. This first exposed card is used as the burn card.

In limit play, the "sevens rule" is assumed to be in use: If a player checks a seven or better and it is the best hand, all action after the draw is void, and he/she cannot win any money on any subsequent bets. If there is an all-in bet after the draw that is less than half a bet, a seven or better may just call and win that bet. However, if another player overcalls this short bet and loses, the person who overcalls receives the bet back. If the seven or better completes to a full bet, this fulfills all obligations.

Deuce-to-Seven Lowball
In deuce-to-seven lowball (sometimes known as Kansas

City lowball), the worst conventional poker hand wins. Straights and flushes count against the hand. The ace is used only as a high card. Therefore, the best hand is 7-5-4-3-2, not all of the same suit. The hand 5-4-3-2-A is not considered to be a straight, but an ace-5 high, so it beats other ace-high hands and pairs, but loses to king-high. A pair of aces is the highest pair, so it loses to any other pair.

The rules for deuce-to-seven lowball are the same as those for ace-to-five lowball, except:

a. The best hand is 7-5-4-3-2 of at least two different suits. Straights and flushes count against the hand, and aces are considered high only;
b. Before the draw, an exposed card of 7, 5, 4, 3, or, 2 must be taken. Any other exposed card must be replaced (including a 6);
c. Check-raise is allowed on any hand after the draw;
d. After the draw, a seven or better is not required to bet.

Badugi (also known as *Badougi*, *Paduki*, *Padooki*)
Most commonly played as a limit game, with a small and big blind; but can be also played as pot limit or no-limit.

Each player is dealt four cards, followed by a round of betting. Then, beginning from the player closest to the left of the dealer, a draw is made. Players may exchange any number of their cards. Badugi is a draw variant of lowball, in which aces are low and the best hand is A-2-3-4 of four different suits. (Any hand containing the four suits is called a badugi). A hand in which one suit, or rank, is duplicated (i.e. a three-card hand) will lose to any badugi. A hand in which two suits or ranks are duplicated will lose to any three-card hand. In the event of a tie, the competing hands are compared, with any duplicates disregarded and the pot being awarded to the player whose hand contains the lowest high card. If there is a tie for the highest card, the second highest card is compared, and so forth. Suit ranking does not apply in the event of a tie.

Pot-Limit Rules

A bet may not exceed the pot size. The maximum amount a player can raise is the amount in the pot after the call is made. Therefore, if a pot is $100, and someone makes a $50 bet, the next player can call $50 and raise the pot $200, for a total bet of $250.

In pot-limit, a player who puts a chip larger than the pot size into the pot without comment is considered to be making a bet of the pot size (unless he/she is facing a bet).

Seats

When a button game starts, active players will draw a card for the button position. The button will be awarded to the highest card by suit for all high and high-low games, and to the lowest card by suit for all low games.

Raising

In no-limit and pot-limit games, unlimited raising is allowed.

In limit poker, for a pot involving three or more players who are not all-in, these limits on raises apply:

a. A game with three or more betting rounds allows a maximum of a bet and three raises;
b. A game with two betting rounds (such as lowball or draw) allows a maximum of a bet and four raises.

In limit play, an all-in bet of less than half a raise does not re-open the betting for any player who has already acted and is in the pot for all previous bets. A player who has not yet acted (or had the betting reopened to him by another player's action), facing an all-in wager of less than half a bet, may fold, call, or complete the wager. An all-in wager of a half a bet or more is treated as a full bet, and a player may fold, call, or make a full raise. (An example of a full raise on a $20 betting round is raising a $15 all-in bet to $35). Multiple all-in wagers, each of an amount too small to individually qualify as a raise, still act as a raise and reopen the betting if the resulting wager size to a player qualifies as a raise.

Odd Chip

If two or more hands tie, an odd chip will be awarded as follows:

a. In a button game, the first hand clockwise from the button gets the odd chip;

b. In a stud game, the odd chip will be given to the highest card by suit in all high games, and to the lowest card by suit in all low games;

c. In high-low split games, the high hand receives the odd chip in a split between the high and the low hands. The odd chip between tied high hands is awarded as in a high game, and the odd chip between tied low hands is awarded as in a low game. If two players have identical hands, the pot will be split as evenly as possible;

d. All side pots and the main pot will be split as separate pots, not mixed together.

Match Poker

Preface

A deep-stack Texas hold 'em tournament is certainly a contest of skill, but there's enough luck involved that just about any decent player is capable of making the money or even finishing first. Think of Jerry Yang, Rob Varkonyi or Hal Fowler, three inexperienced amateurs who managed to win not just a tournament but the championship event of the World Series of Poker. I myself finished fifth in the very first tournament I entered, which happened to be the 2000 WSOP main event. How much luck was involved? Tons and tons.

Match Poker is a variant of no-limit hold 'em from which nearly all of the luck has been drained. The IFP is proud to be introducing it as the Mind Sports version of the world's favorite card game. We have borrowed the concept from Duplicate Bridge. Using decks pre-ordered by shuffling machines or computers, every player is dealt the same cards in the course of a tournament, and their scores reflect how well or poorly they've played them. It's the variant that best guarantees that the smartest, toughest players or teams will win in the short run as well as the long run. The bad news for me is that I never will threaten to win the Match Poker World Championship. The good news is that IFP's Nations Cup will reveal which country has fielded the very best players.

In IFP Match events, the same order of cards is dealt at all tables. Every player in a given seat position across the tournament receives exactly the same cards as his/her fellow competitors in that seat position. The player's skill in playing these hands, in out-performing the other players in the same seat position, determines his/her order of finish. The strength or weakness of the hands will not influence a player's/team's chance to win. In fact, all players in a given seat may be dealt a series of such terrible cards that it would be impossible for them to even make the money in a traditional tournament, let alone win it. But in a Match event, the winning player/team may well be the one that manages to lose the fewest chips with the rags they keep finding when they peer between their knuckles. It will also be up to players to rake the most chips with their monsters.

For traditional poker players, little adjustment is needed to successfully compete in a Match tournament. Each hand, in isolation, is still a hand of no-limit Texas hold 'em in which the player is looking to minimize loss or maximize value . . .

In traditional poker, five critical factors are determined by chance: the strength of one's hole cards; the position in which they are received; their connection to the flop, turn and river; the quality of one's opponents at the table, as well as the hands they are dealt. In Match, such factors are distributed equally–even, one might say, democratically. Fair's fair, after all. At the same, time, you'll never have to–or get to–complain about how unlucky you were. The seating, dealing and scoring systems for individual and team events are described in the pages that follow.

As ambassador for this worthy new variant, I invite you to try your hand in a Match game at the next Nations Cup qualifying satellite. As we all try to outskill the world, may the best team, the best players, win.

As IFP President Anthony Holden likes to put it: "Do not shuffle up, but please deal!"

James McManus
IFP Ambassador for Match Poker,
International Federation of Poker

IFP RULES FOR MATCH POKER

In Match Poker tournaments, the same order of cards (deck-order) is used at all tables. Every player in a given seat position across the tournament receives exactly the same cards as his/her fellow competitors in that seat position. The skill in playing these hands and outperforming the other players in the same seat determines his/her finishing position. In no way does the quality of the cards that players receive influence their chance to win the tournament. Indeed, all players in a given seat may receive such poor cards as to render them unable to win if they were competing in a regular poker tournament. In this situation in a Match Poker tournament, the winning player will be the one that manages to lose the fewest chips with the cards dealt.

Each hand, in isolation, is still a hand of no-limit Texas hold 'em and a player is still looking to win the most (or lose the fewest) chips he/she can on that given hand.

Match Poker is most often played as a team game: each member of a team will be allocated a different seat and will be playing against members of other teams who have also been allocated that seat.

Preparation of Decks

Prior to the tournament, a random number generator is used to generate the required number of deck-orders for the tournament. For example, a single tournament group stage might be played over 150 hands. These deck-orders can be transmitted in encrypted form to a dealing machine that can reliably and automatically sort decks of cards into the required order. Each deck-order (1-150) will need to be duplicated for every table in the tournament. For example, a six table tournament played over 150 hands will require a total of 900 decks. Each deck leaves the dealing machine security-sealed and ready for delivery to the tables. No human eyes need ever see the deck-orders prior to the security seal being broken by the dealer to commence the hand.

Capped No-Limit betting structure and scoring

To preserve fairness and the integrity of the Match Poker concept, in every hand each team must always have a chance to win or lose as many chips as the other teams and so must begin each hand with the same number of chips. The maximum number of chips a player may commit to the pot on any one hand (the cap) is set at 100 times the big blind. Once a player has committed this number of chips to the pot, he/she is all -in. A player may not commit more chips than the cap to any pot, nor may he start a hand with fewer chips than the cap in play. If a player's stack falls below 100 big blinds during the session, the dealer may provide the player with reserve chips.

On each hand, a player will have a net change of chips – negative if he/she commits chips to the pot and does not win; zero if he/she folds without committing chips; and positive if he/she wins the pot. This is his/her chip-score for that hand. The sum of these chip-scores over the session is the player's total chip-score. The total chip-scores of the six players in the Seat 1 position are compared, and points (six for 1st, five for 2nd, four for 3rd, three for 4th, two for 5th and one for 6th) are awarded to each team for their player's performance. The same points structure is applied to the contests in all the other seat positions similarly, and the total points across all six seats determines the ranking of teams in the tournament. In the event of a tie, the chip-scores of the six players on each team are added and the team with the highest aggregate chip-score is the winner (akin to goal-difference in football league tables).

In order to score Match Poker, a console has been designed that allows a tournament official to input the actions of all players at the table (checks, bets, calls, raises and folds) along with the bet amount on each round and the subsequent winner of the pot. These pads communicate directly with a real-time scoring system that displays in-running scores for each seat position and the current standing of the teams.

Security procedure

Knowledge of the cards in play at one table in the Match Poker tournament gives a player knowledge of the exact cards in play at all the other tables in the tournament. For this reason, it is imperative that no communication is allowed between tables. If space allows, tables from the same group (playing the same deck-orders) should be situated in different rooms. In smaller events with the tables in the same room, precautions must be taken to prevent information being exchanged between tables.

There must be no clear line of sight between tables. This can be achieved by placing screens between tables to prevent a player from seeing any cards in play at another table. Further, players may not comment about the specifics of the hand in play. Even after a hand is complete, no player may mention the cards in play, the betting patterns of the other players or the result of the hand. To reduce to an acceptable minimum the information transfer between tables from general noise, the hands in the session should be played in different random orders at each table. In a 75-hand session, all tables must play and complete the same 75 hands, with the button in the same position on each hand as at all other tables; but the order of the hands must be random. A player picking up general noise from the nearby tables will not know which hand is in play at that table and will not be able to infer any useful information.

YOU ARE THE TOURNAMENT DIRECTOR

PREFACE

As a kid I lapped up everything to do with football and I loved the "You are the Ref" comic strip that helped explain the complexities of the game. So when Joe Beevers came up with the idea of a *You Are The Tournament Director* feature for the Hendon Mob website I got it immediately. (Although I still think we should have used little drawings of Matt Savage glaring sternly at errant players, with diagrams showing the position and movement of chips, cards and dealers).

Poker is played everywhere, from Helsinki and Dublin to Atlantic City and Melbourne and of course there are variations in rules, as well as cultural differences around such things as speech play and etiquette. But even with uniform rules, clearly written and perfectly understood, Tournament Directors face new challenges every day.

They rule on incidents they didn't see, and which by definition are open to interpretation and dispute. It can be hard enough to establish what actually took place and who said what, but they may also have to take a view on such intangibles as tone and intention. It may not even be clear which rule or rules should be applied.

Tournament Directors understand what we poker players also know, that poker, particularly in its live form, is situational and interpretative. And that this is as true for them as it is for us. They need to appreciate the difference between a "move" and a "stroke", to define and hold the ethical line between cunning and mendacity, to catch the angle-shooters and protect the inexperienced.

Right from the start, the world's best Tournament Directors threw themselves whole-heartedly into the project, and we are grateful for the trouble they continue to take to explain their well-considered and often conflicting rulings. Almost all the scenarios are real. Some, like the hand in number twenty-four, are celebrated or notorious televised incidents; many more are submitted to us by players and card room staff; all are enthusiastically debated on the Hendon Mob forum. We thank everyone and invite you to carry on making the contributions that have made *You Are The Tournament Director* so popular, respected and widely published.

I salute the efforts of the IFP in creating a definitive book of poker rules, but that is not the end of it. Our panel of Tournament Directors are poker's supreme court, their deliberations and verdicts amounting to a comprehensive body of case law, all of which resides on thehendonmob.com. Essential reading for anyone involved in the live game. In writing the "Mob verdicts" it's wonderful to get the benefit of all their wisdom and experience, and then to have the last word. But of course, there never will be a last word, which is why in our beautiful game, just as in football, being the "b-----d in the black" is the toughest job of all.

Barny Boatman
Poker Player and Co-founder of "The Hendon Mob"

Hendon Mob *You Are The Tournament Director* **case studies, with references to IFP rules.**

Answers begin on page 111

1. Does the Best Hand Always Win?

In a Pot-limit Omaha final there are six players left. Two players are all-in pre-flop with the same number of chips, let's call them Player A and Player B. Player A is a well-respected local player and Player B is generally disliked and a known stroke-puller. Player A's hand is A, K, 7, 8 and player B has A, Q, 7, 8.

The flop came down 10, 10, 10. As the turn card was dealt Player B rose from his seat and started shouting, "Queen, Queen, Queen". The turn was a deuce. Player B continued, louder and louder, "Queen, Queen, Queen." The river card was dealt–it was a queen. The player started shouting "Yes, Yes, Yes" and turned to some friends in the crowd and starting slapping hands and jumping up and down. The dealer pushed the pot to Player B and Player A got up and left the table.

About an hour later Player A was in the bar telling his "bad beat" story when a friend pointed out that he had had the winning hand, three tens with an Ace, King. Player A returns to the final table to find Player B now three handed with a big chip lead. Do you step in?

2. A Fouled Deck

In a Seven-Card stud competition in Russia two players go to war and a big pot develops. Whoever wins this pot will be chip leader going into the final. At the showdown Player A has an ace flush in hearts. Player B also has an ace flush in hearts. Player A's next highest heart is the King, whilst player B's is a Jack. How do you rule and why?

3. Playing Three-Card Omaha

In a $5000 pot limit Omaha competition Player A calls, Player B raises and then Player A re-raises the pot, at which point Player A realizes that he only has three cards. How do you rule?

4. Exposing Your Hand

During a $1000 no-limit hold 'em freeze out we are down to two tables and a pot develops. On the flop Player A bets and Player B moves all-in. Player A starts to think and then turns over his two hole cards to get a reaction from his all-in opponent. How do you rule?

5. Exposing Cards in Error

A situation happened in the EPT event in Vienna in March 2005. Player A raised pre-flop with pocket jacks and got three callers including Player B. The flop came down Q, 10, 2 and Player A bet out. Player B was the only caller. The turn came a Jack, Player B checked and Player A checked behind him. On the river a blank came and Player B bet $500 into a pot of about $2,500. Player

A didn't like it but decided to raise and threw out two $500 chips. Player B (who didn't realize Player A had raised) turned his hand over without calling the raise, he had the nuts–Ace King. How do you rule and why?

6. Verbal Action Away from the Table

We are in the later stages of the WSOP main event, just a few places off the money. The button raises pre-flop and the big blind calls. The flop comes down 10, 6, 10. The big blind bets out, the button makes a big raise and the big blind moves all-in. The button jumps up from his seat and moves away to a nearby wall where he stands with his head in his hands for over a minute. You approach him and explain that he has to make a decision. He says "fold, fold, fold" and then moves back to the table. He looks at the chip stacks and notices that his opponent has a lot of small denomination chips. He realizes that the final re-raise is only a small percentage of the previous bets and now a call is a distinct possibility. He asks for a count of his opponents stack. What do you do?

7. Deals and Collusion

In a pot limit hold 'em competition there are six players left in the final and first prize is about $50,000 which is top heavy at over 50% of the prize pool. Player A is chip leader with about 40% of the chips and the other five players want to discuss a deal to flatten out the prize structure. Player A refuses but the others still want to do a deal. The other five openly say that they will split any prize money that they receive. How do you rule?

8. Chips in Play or Not?
A player sits down in a no-limit hold 'em cash game with an MP3 player, a coffee and a packet of cigarettes. He puts his chips on the table and plays a few hands. The chips in front of him amount to about $1500. He passes for a few minutes until he gets involved in a big pot heads up. He bets $500 and his opponent raises $1000 announcing that he wants to set him in. The new player, who has the nuts by the way, now produces a $5000 chip that was behind his cigarette packet. His opponent objects. How do you rule?

9. I've Got Aces and I'm All-In!
On the bubble in a big NLH competition Player A makes a big raise under the gun. The button moves all-in announcing, "I've got aces, you had better pass if you want to make the money, punk!" You are called to the table, how do you rule?

10. Flop, Turn and River
a. Three players contest a pot pre-flop. Player A bets, Player B calls and before Player C can act, the dealer deals the first card of the flop. How do you rule?
b. Three players contest a pot on the flop. Player A bets, Player B calls and before Player C can act the dealer exposes the turn card. How do you rule?
c. Three players contest a pot on the turn. Player A bets, Player B calls and before Player C can act the dealer

exposes the river card. How do you rule?

11. Leaving Your Seat
In a no-limit hold 'em tournament a player raises and another player then re-raises all-in. As the original raiser is taking an eternity to decide whether or not to call, the all-in player informs the dealer that he is going to the toilet, to which neither dealer nor player voiced an objection. A minute or so later, however, the original raiser summoned the TD for a ruling, claiming that the all-in player had folded by virtue of leaving his seat. How would you rule?

12. I Do Not Fold
Player A goes all-in on the river in a multi-way pot. Everyone else folds. Player B thinks about it, then says, "I do not fold," and flips over his cards. Player A shows his hand: four of a kind, which beats Player B's pair of aces. Player A reaches for the chips, but the other players protest that Player B hadn't called. How would you deal with a player making the verbal declaration "I do not fold" and then exposing his hole cards in a tournament?

13. Mucked in Error
During a big no-limit hold 'em freeze out the action passes to a lady in the one seat who picks up her entire stack, moves it forward over and past her cards and announces herself all-in. She has about seven or eight big blinds. The dealer picks her cards up and puts them

on top of the muck, which comprises four other cards. He releases her cards although they are not shuffled together with the other discards. She screams that she is all-in and he then picks her cards up off the top of the muck and gives them back to her, she peeks at them and nods. One of the players at the table who is still to act asks you for a ruling.

14. If You Raise I Will Go All-In
In a tournament the action is folded to Player A on the small blind. He reaches for his chips and the big blind announces "If you raise, I will go all-in". Player A raises; Player B folds. Should Player B be forced to go all-in after verbally declaring that he would if player A raised?

15. Dead Button and the Blinds
Big blind busts out in a hand, creating a dead button. However, rather than posting a single big blind, the player posts a small blind and the next player posts the big. First player to speak folds and the next player says "raise". The player who folded then calls "time" and points out the mistake with the blinds and suggests that the blinds are corrected and the player who posted the big blind in error should get his blind back and his chance to act first. The player who was originally planning to raise calls for a ruling on the basis that action has taken place (it subsequently turns out, no surprise, that he had a big hand and was scared that a misdeal was being called). How would you rule? Would

you continue the hand or put the blinds right?

16. When is Verbal Action Valid?

During the Monte Carlo Millions it was approaching the end of the day and a player had just lost a big pot. As the dealer started to shuffle he announced that, "When it gets to me I am all-in whatever happens". He still had quite a decent stack.

He said it again as the dealer finished shuffling. Again after the cut. Again after the first card had been dealt. Again after everyone had one card and finally just after the last card had been dealt.

What are his options when the action gets to him? In any event it passed to him, he moved all-in and everyone behind him passed.

17. Another Muck Question

Two players are heads up in a no-limit hold 'em tournament. Player A moves all-in on the river and Player B (who has him covered) calls. Player B then throws his cards face-up on the table revealing the nuts. He throws the cards down with such force that they slide across the table into the muck. You are called to the table and see where Player B's cards appear to have ended up. One of them is deep into the muck so that only a corner is showing; the other is on top of the discards. They are the only two cards which are face-up and the dealer says he believes they are the two cards from Player B's hand. How do you rule?

18. We Should Check This Out
In a no-limit hold 'em tournament a player holding 9, 9 moves all-in for about $500 chips. They are called by two players each of who have about $1,500 chips in total.

They both check the flop and before the turn card is dealt one of them says, "I think we should check this out". The other one says "OK" and they both expose their hands.

The all-in player protests but the dealer goes ahead and deals the turn and river cards. The nines were in front but the river is a queen, making one of the other players a bigger pair.

At this point you are called to the table. How do you rule?

19. Soft Play or Must Call?
This one happened at Aspers Casino in Newcastle in the regular Sunday £100 freeze out. There were eleven players left with ten places paid. Blinds were 1,000-2,000 and Player A, in middle position, raises all-in for 2,400. It is passed round to the big blind. Player B in the big blind, who is a friend of Player A, has mountains of chips and is chip leader. Player B makes a small speech along the lines of, "I have a very bad hand", and

deliberately tosses his hand directly into the muck. The dealer suspects collusion and calls you over to handle the situation. What do you say or do?

20. Does Saying "Bet" Indicate a Raise?

No-limit hold 'em freeze out in a UK casino. Player A raises pre-flop, Player B says "bet" and throws in an amount but just not enough to constitute a legal raise. The player who said "bet" was a well known European Pro who claims that his intention was clear and he says that by saying "bet" he was obviously raising but he hadn't seen the original raise. Do you allow him to make the amount up to a legal raise or is he forced to just call?

21. Flopped Too Soon, Does the Raise Stand?

This ruling was made at the Grosvenor Club in Cardiff. Six players in a self-dealt Omaha game. Player Six is dealing, Players Six, One, and Two have 100 each in the pot. Player Three raises to 500, Player Four raises to 1,000, Player Five calls and Player Six (the dealer) passes. Player One calls, Player Two passes. Before Player Three can act, the dealer turns over two cards of the flop and realizes his mistake and replaces them. At which point Player Three re-raises. A ruling was asked for and the card room manager ruled Player Three out of the pot. Player Three is furious, and will not accept this ruling. It was then decided to shuffle the pack and allow the raise to stand. How would you rule?

22. Is Taking Notes in Live Tournaments Allowed?

A studious player likes to have a pen and paper on the table to make notes about some of the key hands of the tournament. A floor man comes over to warn him to stop writing as it is against the rules. The player asks to speak to a supervisor to get confirmation of this ruling, which he does: the TD explains that taking notes is an unfair advantage against other players and if he persists in doing it, he would suffer a one-orbit penalty. Is note-taking against the rules? How would you rule?

23. The Rivercard is Face-Up

There is a 5/10 no-limit hold 'em cash game. The flop and the turn card are dealt correctly and bets are completed. The dealer discards the burn card to deal the river card, but the river card is face-up in the deck. Does this river card play? Is it a foul deck? How would you rule?

24. Who Wins the Pot and Why?

During an EPT Player A and Player B got involved in a pot when they were both on the blinds. Following action on all streets Player B check called an 80,000 bet from Player A. Player A said "king high" and flashed a king. Player B sat and waited for Player A to show his second card. Player A did not turn over both his cards but instead pushed them over the line and towards the muck. They went into the muck but the dealer retrieved them and turned them both over. There is no doubt that the two cards were Player A's. Player B jumped up and turned over Q high (Q6) claiming that Player A had mucked and the pot was his.

25. What are His Options?
The blinds are 50/100 in a no-limit hold 'em tournament –UTG calls 100–UTG+1 (who has 5,000 in chips total) throws in 150 saying nothing–what are his options? And if he then passes and his chips are left in the pot, is action reopened to UTG when action gets back to him?

26. Is this Considered a Verbal Fold?
Two players are left in the hand. Player A bets $100; Player B sighs and says, "You win." Player A takes back his chips and throws in his cards. But before he can drag in the pot, Player B says, "I call." Imagine the fun after that. Is the "you win" considered a verbal fold?

Answers to the You Are The Tournament Director Questions

1. Does the Best Hand Always Win?
The situation is a result of a dealer mistake, a tricky board and the fact that Player B caused confusion. If the TD had been called to the table before the next hand had been dealt (Rule #24: Disputed Pots), then he/she might have been able to verify the players' hands and correctly award the pot to the best hand. However, as several other hands had been played, the mistake cannot be corrected retroactively.

2. A Fouled Deck
(Rule #63: Fouled Deck) The hand will be declared void. All chips given back to the players and a new deck is called for. (In actuality, the TD ruled that the player with the king would win the pot!)

3. Playing Three-Card Omaha
Rule #49: A player must have a valid hand to win the pot.

4. Exposing Your Hand
Rule #67: Exposing Cards: The hand is live, but Player A will receive a time penalty starting from the next hand.

5. Exposing Cards in Error
Player B may call and claim the pot, but Rule #67:

Exposing Cards still applies. Whether intentionally or accidentally, the player will receive a subsequent penalty.

6. Verbal Action Away from the Table
Even away from the table, verbal declarations are binding (Rule #25).

7. Deals and Collusion
Rule #62: Agreement must be unanimous. There can be no deal. The five players should be warned for collusion, and issued penalties if they persist.

8. Chips in Play or Not?
This is why there are to be no "foreign" objects on the poker table (Rule #22). In this case, as Player B has no view of Player A's chips (Rule #21), the $5000 chip does not play.

9. I've Got Aces and I'm All-in!
Verbal telling of hand is a form of exposing cards (Rule #67). After the hand is over, the player's cards should be looked at, if there was no showdown, and if he was accurate, he will receive a penalty.

10. Flop, Turn and River
a. Let Player C act on his hand, then replace the exposed card with the burn card (2 out of 3 flop cards are correct) and deal the flop (turn and river cards are still correct).
b. Let Player C act on his hand – put the exposed card to the side, then burn and deal the river card in the position

of the turn card, then shuffle the exposed card back into the deck and deal the river without the burn card.

c. Let Player C act on his hand–put the exposed card on the side, then shuffle exposed card back into the deck and deal new river card, without burn card.

11. Leaving Your Seat
The original raiser's hand is dead. Players must remain at the table. (Rule #7)

12. I Do Not Fold
Despite the incorrect language, this is unambiguously a call.

13. Mucked in Error
The technical ruling is clear: It is the player's responsibility to protect her hand (when this situation occurs it is nearly always in the seats to the immediate left or right of the dealer). She should have been more careful and as the cards have been completely released into the muck her hand is dead. As there was no action behind her then it would be fair to give her raise back to her and she would lose the amount of the call. But: this is a case where the TD might choose to overrule the technical ruling and allow the all-in to stand. (Rule #52) This can only be done, however, if we can be certain that the player's correct cards were returned to her. Separately, the TD would have to talk to the players whose cards were also mucked and find out what their holdings were.

14. If You Raise I Will Go All-in

This is grey area: table-talk is part of poker. (Rule #68: Conditional Statements should be strongly discouraged). It is almost tantamount to a verbal declaration. The player should be warned, and penalized if he repeats the offense.

15. Dead Button and the Blinds

Substantial Action has taken place (Rule #29), and the hand must stand, and be played to a conclusion. The blinds can be adjusted on the following hand.

16. When is Verbal Action Valid?

In this instance, as no substantial action has taken place, his verbal declaration is binding (Rule #25). Had the situation changed, he could have changed his action.

17. Another Muck Question

The hand is live, and wins the pot; even though they have touched the muck, the cards are still clearly discernible. Warn the player, though, about the exuberance of his card tosses.

18. We Should Check This Out

This is a clear case of collusion. (Rule #71: Ethical Play) The players should each receive a penalty. However, the hand plays out and the pot is awarded to the pair of queens.

19. Soft Play or Must Call?
This is soft play, a form of collusion (Rule #71) and must be punished with a penalty. If the player's hand has not touched the muck, then the TD may inspect the hand and force the player to call. If it is mucked, he should receive a time penalty.

20. Does Saying "Bet" Indicate a Raise?
Verbal declarations are binding (Rule #25). If the amount is 50% or more of a legal raise, he must make it up to a minimum raise; if it is less than 50%, then it is just a call. Proper terminology of "Call" and "Raise" should be used, and the player should receive a warning.

21. Flopped Too Soon, Does the Raise Stand?
Any flop turned too early may not stand. The action has to be finished; the cards, without a burn card, have to be shuffled; and a new flop is to be dealt.

22. Is Taking Notes in Live Tournaments Allowed?
Note taking is allowed, so long as the paper and pen are not on the table. (Rule #22).

23. The Rivercard is Face-Up
The exposed ("boxed") card is a dead card and will be replaced by the next card in the deck and the hand played to completion.

24. Who Wins the Pot and Why?
Player A was naïve, his opponent possibly unethical,

but he has mucked his cards and has lost the hand.

25. What are His Options?
He must make the raise up to the minimum of 200.

26. Is this Considered a Verbal Fold?
If the called player's hand was clearly retrievable, it should be brought back into play. If not, however, as he had technically not folded, the only player with a valid hand would have to be awarded the pot (Rule #49).

THE LAWS OF POKER

Poker is played with a 52-card deck (unless jokers are being used).

Play moves in a clockwise direction.

All poker hands consist of five cards. In some games, such as hold 'em or Omaha, a choice is made of which combination of hole cards and board cards is used to make up the five-card hand; or in Seven-Card Stud, for example, players make the choice of which five of their seven cards will be used to make their hand.

Hand rankings are as follows:

1 Royal Flush

2 Straight Flush

3 Four of a Kind

4 Full House

5 Flush

6 Straight

7 Three of a kind

8 Two Pair

9 One Pair

10 High Card

Glossary

Action: A fold, check, call, bet, or raise.

Advertising: To make a play that creates a deliberate impression to opponents of one's style – such as to make an obvious bluff in the hope that future bets with stronger hands will be called.

Aggressive Action: A bet that could enable a player to win a pot without a showdown.

All-In: When a player has put all his/her chips into the pot during the course of a hand.

Angle/Angle-Shooting: A technically legal but unethical play.

Ante: A prescribed amount posted before the start of a hand by all players.

Big Blind: The larger regular blind in a game.

Blind: A required bet made before any cards are dealt.

Board: Cards face-up on the table common to each of the hands.

Board Card: A community card in the center of the table, as in hold 'em or Omaha.

Boxed Card: A card that appears face-up in the deck where all other cards are face-down.

Broadway: A 10-J-Q-K-A straight.

Bubble: The final place in a tournament before the payout structure is reached.

Burn Card: After the initial round of cards is dealt, the first card dealt in each round is discarded.

Button: A player who is in the designated dealer position.

California Lowball: Ace-to-five lowball with a joker.

Call the Clock: To limit the amount of time an opponent is taking over a decision.

Capped: Describes the situation in limit poker in which the maximum number of raises on the betting round have been reached.

Cards Speak: The face value of a hand in a showdown is the true value of the hand, regardless of verbal announcement.

Check: To waive the right to bet, but to retain the right to act if another player initiates the betting.

Check-Raise: To waive the right to bet until a bet has been made by an opponent, and then to increase the bet by at least an equal amount when it is your turn to act.

Chip-Dumping: Deliberately losing pots to gift chips to another player.

Chop: To split a pot, because of a tie or when playing high-low games.

Collusion: A form of cheating in which two or more players collaborate against another player.

Color Change/Color Up (or Down): A request to change chips from one denomination to another.

Common Card: A card dealt face-up to be used by all players at the showdown in the games of stud poker whenever there are insufficient cards left in the deck to deal each player a card.

Community Cards: The cards dealt face-up in the center of the table that can be used by all players to form their best hand in the games of hold 'em and Omaha. (Also known as the **Board**).

Complete the Bet: To increase a forced bet to a full bet in limit poker.

Continuation Bet: Generally used in flop games to describe the original pre-flop raiser's opening post-flop bet. (Also known as C-bet).

Cut-Off: The position at the table to the right of the button.

Dark: When a player acts without looking at his/her cards or before the next board card is turned.

Dead Button: A dealer button that cannot be advanced because of the elimination of a player.

Dead Card: A card that is not legally playable.

Dead Hand: A hand that is not legally playable.

Deal Twice/Run it Twice: When there is no more betting, agreeing to have the rest of the cards to come determine only half the pot, removing those cards, and dealing again for the other half of the pot. (This procedure is only followed in cash games).

Dealer Button: A flat disk that indicates the player who is in the dealing position for that hand.

Deck: A set of playing-cards. In these games, the deck consists of either:
(1) 52 cards in seven-card stud, hold 'em, and Omaha;
(2) 53 cards (including the joker), often used in ace-to-

five lowball and draw high.

Dirty Stack: When a player's chips contain more than one denomination in a single stack.

Discard(s): In a draw game, to throw cards out of your hand to make room for replacements, or the card(s) thrown away; the muck.

Double Chance: A tournament format in which players have the option, for a set time period, to receive another starting stack of chips if they have lost their first; if they still have chips at the end of the period, they will receive the second stack as an add-on.

Down Cards: Cards that are dealt face-down in a stud game.

Exposed Card: Any card intentionally or accidentally seen by at least one other player at the table.

Face Card: A king, queen, or jack.

Family Pot: When all players present at the table have called the pre-flop bet.

Fixed Limit: In limit poker, a betting structure where the bet size on each round is pre-set.

Flashed Card: A card that is partially exposed.

Flop: In hold 'em or Omaha, the three community cards that are turned after the first round of betting is complete.

Flush: A poker hand consisting of five cards of the same suit.

Fold: To throw a hand away and relinquish all interest in a pot.

Forced Bet: A required bet to start the action on the first betting round (the normal way action begins in a stud game).

Fouled Hand: A dead hand.

Fourth Street: The second up card in seven-card stud or the first boardcard after the flop in hold 'em (also called the **Turn Card**).

Freeroll: A chance to win something at no risk or cost.

Full House: A hand consisting of three of a kind and a pair.

Going South: Surreptitiously taking chips out of one's stack and therefore out of the game.

Hand-for-Hand: As tournaments near final tables and/ or payout places, the TD may dictate hand-for-hand play, in which each hand is begun simultaneously at all tables.

Heads-Up Play: Only two players involved in play.

Hijack: The position at the table two to the right of the button.

Hole Cards: The cards dealt face-down to a player.

Joker: The joker is a "partly wild card" in high draw poker and ace-to-five lowball. In high, it is used for aces, straights, and flushes. In lowball, it is the lowest unmatched rank in a hand.

Kansas City Lowball: A form of draw poker low also known as deuce-to-seven, in which the best hand is 7-5-4-3-2 and straights and flushes count against the hand.

Kicker: The highest unpaired card that helps determine the value of a five-card poker hand.

Live Blind: A blind bet giving a player the option of raising if no-one else has raised.

Lowball: A draw game where the lowest hand wins.

Lowcard: At seven-card stud, the lowest up card, which is required to bet.

Miscall: An incorrect verbal declaration of the ranking of a hand.

Misdeal: A mistake on the dealing of a hand which causes the cards to be reshuffled and a new hand to be dealt.

Missed Blind: A required bet that is not posted when it is a player's turn to do so.

Monster: A hugely powerful starting hand.

Muck: (1) noun - The pile of discards gathered facedown in the center of the table by the dealer. (2) verb - To discard a hand.

No-Limit: A betting structure allowing players to bet any amount of their chips in one bet.

Nuts: The best possible hand.

Opener: The player who made the first voluntary bet.

Opener Button: A button used to indicate who opened a particular pot in a draw game.

Openers: In jacks-or-better draw, the cards held by the player who opens the pot that show the hand qualifies to be opened.

Option: The choice to raise a bet given to a player with a blind.

Orbit: A full rotation of the table.

Out of Position: When a player is not the last to act in a betting round.

Overblind: Also called oversize blind. A blind used in some pots that is bigger than the regular big blind, and usually increases the stakes proportionally.

Pair: Two cards of the same rank.

Pass: (1) Decline to bet (**Check**). (2) Decline to call a wager, at which point the player must discard the hand and have no further interest in the pot (**Fold**).

Pat/Stand Pat: Not drawing any cards in a draw game.

Play Behind: To have chips in play that are not in front of the player (allowed only when waiting for chips that are already purchased).

Play Over: To play in a seat when the occupant is absent.

Play the Board: Using all five community cards for the hand in hold 'em.

Playover Box: A clear plastic box used to cover and protect the chips of an absent player when someone plays over that seat.

Position: (1) The relation of a player's seat to the blinds or the button. (2) The order of acting on a betting round or deal.

Postillion/Cut Card: The plastic card that is used by the dealer to conceal the bottom of the deck.

Pot-Limit: The betting structure of a game in which you are allowed to bet up to the amount of the pot.

Proposition Bet: A side bet not related to the outcome of the hand.

Protected Hand: A hand of cards that the player is physically holding, or has topped with a chip or some other object to prevent a fouled hand.

Push: When a new dealer replaces an existing dealer at a particular table.

Quads: Four of a kind.

Rabbit Hunting: The practice of continuing to deal the deck or the board, to see which cards would have been exposed, after the pot has been awarded.

Rack: (1) A container in which chips are stored while being transported. (2) A tray in front of the dealer, used to hold chips and cards.

Rags: Insignificant cards of low value.

Raise: To increase the amount of a previous wager. This increase must meet certain specifications, depending on the game, to reopen the betting and count toward a limit on the number of raises allowed.

Rankings: Poker follows bridge suit ranking: the order, from the highest down, is spades, hearts, diamonds, clubs. Ranking can be used in the event of a tie to determine the winner of a chip race, when allocating a seat, or determining the recipient of an odd chip. It may never be used to influence or determine the awarding of a pot.

Re-raise: To raise an opponent's raise. Often known as a three-bet.

Royal Flush: A-K-Q-J-10 all of the same suit.

Satellite: A tournament in which the prize is entry to a larger tournament.

Scoop: To win the entire pot in a high-low split game.

Set: Three of a kind; in hold 'em, usually the term for

when a player has two of the cards in his/her hand.

Setup: Two new decks, each with different colored backs, to replace the current decks.

Shootout: A tournament in which the last remaining player at each table goes on to play the last remaining players of other tables.

Shove: To move all-in.

Showdown: The showing of cards to determine the pot-winner after all the betting is over.

Shuffle: The act of mixing the cards before a hand.

Side Pot: A separate pot formed when one or more players are all-in.

Slow Roll: To delay showing the winning hand—a major breach of etiquette.

Small Blind: In a game with multiple blind bets, the smaller blind.

Soft Play: A form of collusion in which one player intentionally goes easy on another player.

Splashing the Pot: To put, or throw, chips directly into the pot when making a bet, making it difficult for the dealer and the other players to verify the amount of chips wagered. The correct procedure is for a player to move the chips towards the pot while keeping them separate.

Split Pot: A pot that is divided among players, either because of a tie for the best hand or by agreement prior to the showdown.

Splitting Openers: In high draw jacks-or-better poker, dividing openers in hopes of making a different type of hand (such as breaking aces to draw at a flush).

Stack: Chips in front of a player.

Straddle: An additional, optional blind bet placed after the forced blinds, usually double the big blind in size, giving the player the option to raise if the action comes back unraised.

Straight: Five cards in consecutive rank.

Straight Flush: Five cards in consecutive rank of the same suit.

Street: Cards dealt on a particular round. For example, the fourth card in a player's hand in stud is often known as fourth street.

String Bet: An illegal bet made in more than one delivery

of chips, without prior announcement of the amount
to be bet.

Stub: The portion of the deck which has not been dealt.

Table Stakes: The amount of money a player has on the
table. This is the maximum amount that a player can
wager or lose on a hand.

Time: An announcement used to stop the action on a
hand.

Trips: Three of a kind; in hold 'em, the term usually
used for when the player has one of the cards in his/her
hand, with two on the board.

Turn Card: The fourth street card in hold 'em or
Omaha.

Under the Gun: The position at the table immediately
to the left of the big blind, and therefore first to act in
forced blind games such as hold 'em and Omaha.

Up Cards: Cards that are dealt face-up for opponents
to see in stud games.

Vigorish/Vig/Juice: The rake or amount of money that
the establishment takes to provide the service of poker.

Acknowledgments

We stand on the shoulders of giants. The IFP committee studied pre-existing rulebooks to compile these sets of rules. The very well thought-through, and tested, TDA (Tournament Directors Association), WSOP (World Series of Poker), EPT (European Poker Tour), BSOP (Brazilian Series of Poker), APSA (Austrian Pokersport Association) and FIDPA (Fédération Internationale de Poker Association) sets of rules were drawn upon, to create what we hope is the most comprehensive and authoritative tournament rulebook available. Some original wording from those pre-existing rules were used and proper credit should be given to their authors.

For the cash games and glossary sections, the invaluable work of Robert Ciaffone (*Robert's Rules of Poker*) has been drawn upon.

And, we are indebted to the Hendon Mob for being allowed to use case studies from its website's regular feature, *You Are The Tournament Director*.

NOTES

NOTES